WHAT DOES IT DO? WHAT DOES IT DO? WHAT DOES IT DO?
WHAT DOES IT DO?
WHAT DOES IT DO?
WHAT DOES IT DO?
WHAT DOES IT DO?
WHAT DOES IT DO?

COMMUNITY · CONNECTIONS

?

WHAT DOES IT DO?
WINDMILL

BY MARK FRIEDMAN

CHERRY LAKE
Publishing

Published in the United States of America by Cherry Lake Publishing
Ann Arbor, Michigan
www.cherrylakepublishing.com

Content Adviser: Louis Teel, Professor of Heavy Equipment, Central Arizona College

Photo Credits: Cover and page 1, ©Pati Photo/Shutterstock, Inc.; page 5,
©visdia/Shutterstock, Inc.; page 7, ©iStockphoto.com/JoeGough; page 9,
©iStockphoto.com/bronswerk; page 11, ©Media Union/Shutterstock, Inc.;
page 13, ©iStockphoto.com/Freezingtime; page 15, ©Michaela Stejskalova/
Shutterstock, Inc.; page 17, ©iStockphoto.com/josiephos; page 19, ©iStockphoto.com/
kruwt; page 21, ©Greg Wright/Alamy

Copyright ©2012 by Cherry Lake Publishing
All rights reserved. No part of this book may be reproduced or utilized in any form
or by any means without written permission from the publisher.

LIBRARY OF CONGRESS CATALOGING-IN-PUBLICATION DATA
Friedman, Mark, 1963–
  What does it do? Windmill/by Mark Friedman.
     p. cm.—(Community connections)
  Includes bibliographical references and index.
  ISBN-13: 978-1-61080-118-8 (lib. bdg.)
  ISBN-10: 1-61080-118-0 (lib. bdg.)
  1. Windmills—Juvenile literature. 2. Wind power plants—Juvenile literature.
  I. Title. II. Title: Windmill. III. Series.
  TJ825.F73 2011
  621.4'53—dc22   2011000259

Cherry Lake Publishing would like to acknowledge the
work of The Partnership for 21st Century Skills. Please
visit www.21stcenturyskills.org for more information.

Printed in the United States of America
Corporate Graphics Inc.
July 2011
CLFA09

CONTENTS

4 **What Is a Windmill?**

8 **How Does a Windmill Work?**

14 **Types of Windmills**

18 **Where Are Windmills?**

22 Glossary

23 Find Out More

24 Index

24 About the Author

WHAT DOES IT DO?

WHAT IS A WINDMILL?

Have you ever seen a **wind farm**? Power companies build wind farms to **harvest** wind energy. Windmills use this wind energy to produce electricity. This electricity powers our homes and businesses.

Wind farms are made up of many windmills arranged in rows.

LOOK!

Take a close look at a wind farm. Notice how the windmills are placed. Do you think the wind farm looks like a farm that grows food? Explain why or why not.

5

Windmills stand at the tops of tall towers. They face the direction of the wind.

The windmill's **rotors** turn when the wind blows against them. The turning rotors help turn wind energy into electricity.

Do you see the windmill's rotors?

HOW DOES A WINDMILL WORK?

Windmills have three main parts. They are rotors, a **shaft**, and a **generator**.

You have probably seen rotors before. They are metal blades that catch the wind and spin around.

Many windmill rotors look like airplane propellers.

The shaft is a long rod. It is attached to the rotors at one end. The other end is connected to the generator.

The turning rotors make the shaft turn, too. Energy from the shaft is carried to the generator.

The shaft runs through the middle of the box behind the rotors.

You can make your own windmill. Cut a piece of thick paper to create rotors. Use a pin as the shaft. Push the pin through the center of the paper. Then poke it into the eraser end of a pencil. Blow on the rotors to make them turn.

11

The generator is made up of a **conductor** and a ring of magnets. The windmill's shaft is connected to the conductor. The magnets make a ring around it.

The conductor spins as the shaft spins. This generates electricity in the magnets. Cables carry the electricity out of the windmill.

Workers can open up the parts of a windmill to make repairs.

13

TYPES OF WINDMILLS

People have been using windmills for a long time. But they did not always use them to provide electricity.

Farm windmills helped grind wheat and other grains. Windmills were also used to pump water.

The first windmills were built hundreds of years ago.

15

Most windmills today are used to provide electricity. They are often called **wind turbines**. Some of them have long, flat rotors. They look like giant fans.

Others have curved rotors that spin around the shaft. They come in many different shapes.

This windmill has curved rotors.

Other sources of electricity can release harmful gases into the air. But wind power does not. It is good for the environment. What are some other reasons that people might use wind power?

17

WHERE ARE WINDMILLS?

You can find windmills in many places today. Most wind farms are found in big open fields.

Offshore wind farms are built on oceans or lakes. Wind farms are usually built far away from houses because they can be noisy.

Offshore wind farms create electricity without taking up space on land.

19

Some people have their own windmills. Some office buildings and factories also have windmills. These windmills can save people and businesses a lot of money on electricity.

Can you hear the wind blowing? Think about all the energy it can provide!

A small windmill can provide enough electricity to power a home.

Do you think a windmill could power your family's home? Ask your parents if they have ever heard about windmills for homes. They might be able to save money by using wind power!

21

GLOSSARY

conductor (kuhn-DUHK-tur) a coil of wire that creates electricity when it moves inside a ring of magnets

generator (JEN-uh-ray-tur) the part of a windmill that turns wind energy into electricity

harvest (HAR-vist) to gather materials such as crops or wind energy on a farm

offshore (AWF-shor) located in the water but near the coast

rotors (ROH-turz) the blades on a windmill

shaft (SHAFT) the pole on a windmill that connects the rotors to the generator

wind farm (WIND FARM) an area in a field or on a body of water where many windmills are built

wind turbines (WIND TUR-binez) another name for windmills that turn wind energy into electricity

FIND OUT MORE

BOOKS

Dobson, Clive. *Wind Power: 20 Projects to Make with Paper.* Toronto: Firefly Books, 2010.

Walker, Niki. *Generating Wind Power.* New York: Crabtree Publishing, 2007.

WEB SITES

Energy Kids: Renewable Wind
www.eia.doe.gov/kids/energy.cfm?page=wind_home-basics
Get more information about wind power from the U.S. Energy Information Administration.

Science News for Kids: Power of the Wind
www.sciencenewsforkids.org/articles/20050309/Feature1.asp
Read an interesting article about how wind power is used today.

INDEX

blades, 8
businesses, 4, 20

cables, 12
conductor, 12

electricity, 4, 12,
  14, 16, 17, 20
energy, 4, 6, 10

factories, 20
farms, 14

gases, 17
generators, 8, 10, 12
grains, 14

homes, 4, 21

magnets, 12
money, 20, 21

noise, 18

offshore wind
  farms, 18

power companies, 4
pumps, 14

rotors, 6, 8, 10,
  11, 16

shafts, 8, 10, 11,
  12, 16
shapes, 16

towers, 6

water, 14
wind farms, 4, 5,
  18
wind turbines, 16

ABOUT THE AUTHOR

Mark Friedman
has been a writer
and editor of
children's books and
educational materials
for 20 years. He
has written picture
books, biographies,
textbooks, and books
on science concepts,
history, culture,
government, poetry,
holidays, religion,
and more.

24